Right Side Up!

Reflections
for Those Living
with Serious
Illness

Marlene Halpin,
Dominican

Photography and text by Marlene Halpin

Book Team

Publisher: Sandra J. Hirstein
Managing Editor: Mary Jo Graham
Assistant Editor: Sharon K. Cruse
Cover Design: Bob Neumann

Copyright © 1995 by Islewest Publishing,
a division of Carlisle Communications, Inc.
4242 Chavenelle Drive, Dubuque, IA 52002.
Manufactured in the United States of America.
All rights reserved.

ISBN 0-9641919-3-8

Contents

Preface

The Beginning

It was a hospice nurse who, inadvertently, began this book.

After one long day, Hildy sat and sighed. She began talking about one of her hospice patients. This man had, his whole life, been an avid reader. Well-meaning friends, when visiting, brought him books as a gift to help fill his time with pleasure.

Quite the opposite happened.

Not pleasure, but *frustration*, was the effect of their gifts.

Frank has not the strength to hold the books.

Frank no longer has the control to turn pages easily.

Frank can't focus enough to read page after page.

Frank, at this part of his life, is worn out and tired.

However, Frank has his good hours. He is alert sometimes during the day. Conversations, news, ideas give him pleasure.

"Why," asked Hildy, "doesn't someone write a book someone like Frank can manage?"

So *Right Side Up!* began.

What else would Frank, or someone in Frank's stage of life, want?

"Short!" said Hildy. "Beautiful!" said Sandy. "Manageable!" said Janet. "Realistic!" said John. "Very ill people think and feel a great deal. Some of it gets communicated badly because of pain and weariness. Much of it does not get communicated at all because . . . well, it's embarrassing. A good Christian wouldn't say things like that . . . or, you just don't have the strength."

"Besides," Bill added, "people like me worry about being a burden. I'm the *man*. I'm the one to take care of *them*."

"Easy for you to say. When you're stuck in bed you need attention. You want them to know what you're going through. . . . Sometimes it's hard to explain, and they tell you to stop whinning," Emily added.

The Middle

So came a time of listening.

Listening to people who are, or once were, very ill. People who are coming close to death.

Listening to people who care for people who are very ill.

"Whether you say it or not, what concerns you? . . . What is happening to *you* as your body changes? . . . *What do you wish those around you understood about you now, as you are <u>now</u>?*

"Most important of all, as your body begins to shut down, what effect does this have on *your spirit?* . . . What are your worries? . . . What nags at you? . . . What would you like to finish?

"And, for this is so very true, your life as you have known it is coming full circle. Now that you have nothing else to do (because you *cannot* do anything else!) you can attend to your*self.* You aren't busy! (Now that's a different way to live the day!) As your life unclutters (except for the interruptions for medication, or bed pan, or bed bath) you come to the heart of things without hurry. . . . On and off, things might occur to you.

"How does the heart of things, the importance of *yourself,* come to be amid the pain and weariness, the frustrations and fears, the *relentlessness* of being so ill? So *relentlessly* ill?"

These are the things that, in one way or another, were asked and listened to.

The End (which, of course, is a new beginning)

It's uneven, this journey. Some days are good; some aren't. It's uncertain, too. From day to day, there is much that is uncertain.

That's what *life* brings.

What does the *spirit,* that *wonderful spirit* in each human being, make of this part of life? That is up to each one of us!

How do you want what you are going through to end for you?

It really is your decision. What does your intermost heart long for?

Will the uncertainty end in <u>trusting</u>, trusting with a depth and a sureness never known before, in the goodness of a good God who awaits your coming with a most loving welcome?

Will the uncertainty end in <u>contentment</u>, contentment with being aware of your God who made you? Your God who is quite satisfied with you as you are—with all your graces and limitations, failures and goodness? Contentment with yourself, with your spirit now becoming uncluttered, and simply shining in the beauty of your*self* as you never could before?

But now you can.

And hopefully will—
        as your heart wishes,
        as your God wishes.

Upside Down

My World is upside down.

I used to be giving . . .
      now I'm receiving.

I used to be in charge . . .
      now they tell me *what* and *when*.

I used to be in control . . .
      now they talk around me.

I used to be independent . . .
      now I cannot be.

It is all upside down.
      Are there any bright spots in these ways
      I'm not used to?

I suppose if I think about
      being taken care of,
      lacking control and independence,
I suppose it could help me
      to unclutter my life.
I suppose it could free me
      to see who *and* what
      are really important to me.

Please, look with me, and help me
      find what's there for me,

           my God.

Abandoned

They don't answer the bell.
They don't call.
They don't come.
Or, they don't come back.
I feel abandoned.

I know they're busy.
I've been busy, too.
       But, right now, I *need* them.
       I *want* them.
I don't like admitting
how much it means to me.

Maybe they don't realize it.
Maybe I didn't realize it, either, back when . . .

I suppose I'm old enough
to know I don't always get
what I want, or think I need.

I suppose I'm old enough
to know having a pity-party
doesn't help for long.

Am I old enough
to know YOU ARE MY ENOUGH,

               my God?

Are You?

Ever since I was a small child
I was taught
> - to say my prayers,
> - to be good,
> - to please God,

for that was what mattered most.

> As I grew up
> > - sometimes I said my prayers
> > - when in trouble I prayed
> > - and, most of the time,
> > > I tried to be good,
> > > and hoped that it would please God.
> > > (Well, when I thought about it.)

Now, when it seems that soon
I shall die,
> will I really "meet my Maker?"
> Will there be a Maker to meet?
> Suppose God . . . isn't?
> . . . Was all this "being good" worth it?

> > *As I face myself at this ending of my life,*
> > *How do I want to answer these questions?*
> > *And, what do I, down deep,*
> > *think of Your being,*

> > > my God?

Changing

As my mind and heart roam around my life,
It strikes me over and over, how everything changes.

Not just things, people.
Not just people, me.

      I used to be concerned about . . .
      I used to think . . .
      I used to want . . .

      Sometimes I was disappointed.
      Sometimes I was gladdened.

      And now?

Is all this change just change?
Is there anything in it I can count on, always?
Is there anyone I can count on, always?

    (How I *long* for always!)

      As my mind and heart roam about my life,
      I do see an "always,"
      An "always" I didn't always see:

      The "always" of Your presence,
        Your loving, caring presence,

                    my God.

Dying

I've never died before.
How do you <u>do</u> it?

Sometimes I want to die,
       to end all this pain,
       to stop all this bother.

Sometimes I'm afraid.

Sometimes I wonder:
       Am I ready to die?
       Am I doing it right?

> *Help me remember,*
> *please,*
> *how the Bible says*
> *Jesus knew he came from God*
> *and was returning to God.*
>
> *I, too, came from You!*
> *I, too, am coming back to You!*
> *Thank You,*

                 my God.

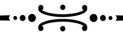

Enough

I love life!
I love people!
I love being alive!

As I live
through my dying,

      am I really,
      really coming to the point
      of *knowing,* way down deep inside,
      knowing

      all
      I have ever loved
      is very good, indeed.

And because of it all,
      through it all,

      Now that we are about to meet,
          face to face,
      I know, as I never knew before,

      Nothing is lost,
      and all is found in You.

      YOU who are my enough,

              my God.

Everyone Tells Me

Everyone tells me what to do.
    They did this—so I should.
    Their cousin did that—so I should.
    Their in-laws didn't do this—so I shouldn't.

I'm tired of everyone telling me what to do!

      They mean to help.
      Maybe it helps them to try to help me.

Let me be at peace with their good will.
Let me be at peace with my own decisions.
Let me be at peace with you,

                     my God.

Forgotten

They don't call.
They don't come.
I feel invisible, forgotten.

I know they are busy.
I've been busy myself.
But . . . it means so much.

Maybe they don't realize it,
as I didn't, back when . . .

But, right now,
I feel forgotten
by those I love most.

Empty,
when I'd rather be full,
is how I come to You
this day,

my God.

Gain and Loss

As a child I learned,
>　*"What profits it a man to gain the whole world,*
>　*and lose his soul?"*

Well,
>　I didn't gain the whole world,
>　nor did I lose my soul.

But,
>　I gained some of the world,
>　and maybe sold some of my soul.

Now?
>　Now I look at those used-to-be-important
>　　　aspects of my life.
>　I look at them with new, perhaps wiser, eyes.

Now?
>　*Now I am asking myself, for one of the last times,*
>　*What's really important to me? What contents me?*
>　*As the pieces of my life fall into place, at last . . .*
>　*I am getting ready for You,*
>　　　　　　　my God.

How Long?

How often, over the years,
have I asked:
      "How long do I wait?"
      "How long will this take?"

And now
I ask it of my dying.

      "How long will it take?"
      "How long will I be here?"

Like a pregnant woman
waiting for her time to come,
Now

      I'm waiting for
      "my time"
      to come
      to be born
      to You,

                    my God.

I Didn't Know

As my mind and heart roam around my life
I am surprised, sometimes;
      chagrined, even, for

    I didn't know
      I didn't have to do that.
    I didn't know
      I didn't have to take that on.
    I didn't know
      what they were really like.
    I didn't know
      how much they cared.
    I didn't know
      it was important. (or not)

Maybe,
      I didn't know myself, either,
      as well as I thought I did.
      Or You . . .

Now,
        I shall, indeed,
        —and with gladness—
        know us both,

                my God.

I Don't . . . I Do!

I get so irritable
nobody knows what I want.
I don't . . . but, I do.

> I do want people around.
> People who know me.
> People who care about me.

I don't want anyone around.
Pain wears me out.
I don't have the energy to talk.
I can't concentrate.

> I do want people around,
> and, I don't.
> I get out of sorts and
> I don't have the energy to explain.

Help them understand,
in spite of my irritation,
I need them.
Silent. Caring.

> *Please,*
> *especially when I am out of sorts,*
> *help them know I want them.*
> *And You,*

> my God.

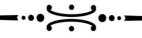

I Don't Like It!

Being like this,
this long,
depresses me.

Will they hold my job? . . . What will I do?
Will my family survive this? . . . How?

My world is falling apart.

Even when people visit me . . .

   - Some are so healthy and busy, they offend me.
   - Some are so worried about me, they burden me.
   - Some are so full of platitudes, they weary me.

I don't like it!

   Yet I need them, them and their visits.

      In truth,
      they are as they are.
      For them it is, perhaps, right.

      In truth,
      I am as I am.
      For me it is right—
      for there is no other way
      for me to be.

*Let me be at peace
        with them, as they are.*

*Let me be at peace
        with me, as I am.*

*Let me be at peace
        with You, as You are,*

my God.

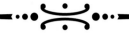

I Love You

As my mind and heart
roam around my life
I realize there are things
       I wish I had done . . .
       I wish I had said . . .
But I didn't.

       Nothing was wrong.
       I just didn't get around to it,
       or I took it for granted.

Oh,
but is there still a chance
I can say,

       I love You.
       I always have.

       I know it.
       And so do You,

         my God.

I'm Too Young to Die

That's it!
I'm just too young to die.

> Why
> am I
> *like this?*
>
> What did I
> ever do
> to deserve *this?*

When I don't get any answers
(like now)
I suspect I'm asking the wrong questions.

> Most people my age don't die.
> I'm not "most people."

> *Could it be*
> *that I am dying*
> *at my age*
> *because <u>You</u> think I'm complete,*
> *for me, now?*
> *Do I <u>really</u> think*
> *my judgment better than Yours,*
> *whether I understand it or not?*
> *Help me! Please, help me,*

> my God.

I Never Knew

I never knew
      how much I took for granted.
I never knew
      how much I never noticed.

Now
      I bask in a real smile.
      I appreciate a cool sip of water,
         one good taste in my mouth.
      I love the play of sunlight on the wall.
      I relish the comforting presence of people.

Now
      I notice the small things.
      Each of them becoming a big thing.

Perhaps
      This is a good way
      to become ready for the biggest event of all:

         Our meeting each other,
         face to face,

               my God.

I Worry

I worry
and
I wish.

> I wish I had taken care of those things
> before I got this sick.
> I worry what will happen to them
> if I don't recover.

I think
> Maybe tomorrow
> I'll have the strength
> to do something about it.

I know
probably
I won't.

> *Help me to be at peace*
> *with all the things*
> *that are left, not done,*

                    my God.

Images

If my soul
        were to
        photograph
my inner life—
        what
        might the image be?

      - And the next one?

      - And the next one?

      - And the next?

Until,
        at long last,
        there is

                my picture,
                my smiling picture,
                with You,
                smiling, too,

                        my God.

Important Things

As my mind and heart roam around my life
I see that different things were important to me
      at different times.

      Once, *this* was important,
      At another time, *that* . . .

      I gave a great deal to succeed in those
            then-important things
      Which hardly can I remember now, but
      Each of which had a part in forming me into
      Me, as I am, now.

What is important now?

            This minute.
            Maybe, the next minute.
            My being.
                  I may not be as I was, but
                  I am!
                  And I am coming to You,

                        my God.

It Could Have Been Different

The "might have beens" . . .
The "could have beens" . . .
The "well, they weren't" things of my life . . .

Why is my life like this?
    The answers are too many.
    And too few.

Who's to blame?
    Me. Them. Us.
    Everyone. No one.

What am I to do?
    Ponder the mystery of it all.
    Somehow, trust God as never before.
    Believe that God's love will make it whole.

So, now:
    As I <u>believe in</u> You,
    As <u>I believe You</u>,
    Make a whole of me
    out of these "might" and "could have" beens,
    out of these "weren'ts," but also
    out of all things that <u>were</u>!
    Please,

                      my God.

"IT"

As my mind and heart roam around my life,
IT keeps coming back.

Over the years, IT has had a way
of coming back to haunt me.

I think I have put IT out of my mind.
And I have, for a while.
Then IT comes back again.
Like now.

I am so sorry about IT.
If I could live IT over,
I'd live IT differently.

But, I can't.

Maybe, at long last,
I know IT is part of my life.

*And so I come with that part, too,
with IT,
as I come, trusting Your mercy,
to You,*

my God.

Lonely

I'm lonely.

Oh, the health professional people come in.
They do what they can to ease and help me.
They are nice.
They don't know me.
       I'm lonely.

Oh, visitors come in.
They ask how I am and
       are glad or sorry according to my response.
They tell me how they are
       often at wearying length.
Or they cry at how I am.
How well do they <u>know</u> how I am?
       I'm lonely.

       There are long times in between.
       Then I wonder
       how I am.

       Or,
       all things considered,
       should I feel like this
       for how I am?

I don't know.

I suppose they do their best
when they visit me.
As I did my best
when I visited others.

For their best I bless them.
For my best bless me,

You who do know me,
You who <u>do know</u> how I am,

my God.

Miss Me!

Will they miss me?

>I hope so!
>But,
>I hope not so much
>that *they* don't *live*!

I hope

>I remain
>in their love
>in their memories
>in their loving and funny stories.

I hope

>losing me like this
>gentles them, in their living.

I really don't like leaving them.

>>*But—*
>>*it is time*
>>*(or close to it)*
>>*and life*
>>*urges me*
>>*to new life*
>>*with You,*

>>>my God.

Moses

As my heart and mind roam around my life
I know that—every so often—
I knew you, my God.

During these days of dying,
Sometimes I come to know you again.

I am happily full of you.
I *long* to be with you.
To enjoy "life in abundance."
Fully.

But someone I love is not yet ready
to let me go.
Or to see that I am ready.

Let me remember Moses who
put a veil over his face
after he saw God.
His face was too bright,
too painfully bright,
for the people to see.

Someone I love cannot bear
that I see You, that I <u>long for</u> You.

Bless them, bless me,
now . . . and then,

my God.

Mourning

I don't have to roam around my mind and heart
to know what I mourn. Or, rather, whom.

> Why is it, sometimes,
>> when I love someone a great deal
>> they seem barely to tolerate me?

> Why is it, sometimes,
>> when someone loves me (maybe a great deal)
>> I have trouble even barely tolerating them?

> Why isn't there a better match?

I don't know.
> I mourn the ones who didn't love me back.
> I mourn for myself that I didn't love
>> those others.

And I need to remind myself:
> God, who cannot be mistaken,
> loves each of us
> with an unconditional love.

> *And I,*
> *I, to be more truthful,*
> *need to love and let myself be loved*
> *as each one can,*
> *including myself,*
> *and You,*

>> my God.

Nagging

Who will take care of them?

That nags at me, tugs at me,
more than anything.

No one can care for them
the way I do.

How will they get along?

>   Yet,
>   I've done what I can,
>   as have they.

>   Maybe
>   not all we'd like,
>   but, under our circumstances,
>   all we could.

>   *Now*
>   *I need to trust them --*
>   *their lives and their goodness--*
>   *to bring them to where I am now:*
>   *ready (well, almost ready)*
>   *to be with You,*

>   my God.

Pain

How can somebody else
<u>really know</u>
what my pain is like?
> - how it invades me
> - how it plays unexpected games with me
> - how now it is worse, now a little less so

Do they at least
> <u>really know</u>
> it isn't that I don't care about them,
> or that I don't want to talk with them
> or listen to them
> but that my pain uses up all of my attention?

> > *Let me be at peace*
> > *in <u>Your</u> ever-present presence,*
> > *for I know*
> > *<u>You</u> do know,*

> > > my God.

People

As my mind and heart roam around my life,
I think about,
> see,
> hear,
> feel,
> smell,
the people who inhabited it.

> Some—at one time or another,
> Some—now and then,
> Some—rather constantly present, for a time,
> Some—with me, almost forever.

> > *Those who peopled my life*
> > *(I think of each gently, now)*
> > *Blessed me . . . in one way or another,*
> > *By who and how they were . . .*
> > > *and are.*

Now
> > *I bless them . . . in one way or another*
> > *and ask You*
> > *to bless us all,*
> > > > my God.

Questions

Always
I had so many questions.

Almost always
I'd fret
until I had answers.

>   Now
>   I know
>   I don't know the answers.
>   And I know
>   No one else does, either.
>
>   Most of all,
>   I now know
>   I don't have to know.

>   *Help me, please,*
>   *to live the mystery of living,*
>   *to live the mystery of dying,*
>   *to live the mystery of new life*
>   *with You,*

>   my God.

Separation

Always

there have been separations:
- at births
- leaving home
- finishing school
- changing jobs
- launching children

Separations followed by:
- new ways of living
- new work
- new experiences

The lists could go on and on.

> *May this impending separation*
> *of me from this earth*
> *begin*
> *a brand new*
> *way of living*
> *with You,*

my God.

Sin

Those things I did (or left undone)
        wrongly—knowingly and willingly
I am responsible for
        seeking Your forgiveness
        and making what amends I can.

Those things I did (or left undone)
        with neither thought nor conscious will
        but which were hurtful
        (as I sometimes later found out)

For these
        careless and unwitting sins of mine
        I also seek Your forgiveness
        and will,
        by my love and prayer,
        make what amends I can.

                But—
                oh,
                how I count on
                Your mercy,

                    my God.

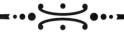

Tears in My Heart

No matter how bad
  my body's pain
It's next to nothing
  compared to the
  pain in my heart.

How do I say
  "good-bye"
knowing there's no
  "hello"
  to come again on this earth?

Good-bye
  to my life
  to my hopes and dreams
  to all of you whom I love.

This is the worst,
  the very worst,
  pain.

    So I come
    with tears filling
    my throat and my heart.
    I come
    with lonely desolation
    of having nothing left.

    . . . What will You do with me,

      my God?

The Things I Did!

As my mind and heart roam around my life
I think of the things I did.
And those I didn't.

     Good and not-so-good, those I did.
     Good and not-so-good, those I didn't do.

I seem to remember
that when Jesus spoke
to the Woman at the Well
He told her *everything* she ever did:
        - every good thing
        - every regrettable thing
        - every public thing
        - every private thing
        - every wonderful, loving thing!
Everything!

       My everything?
       Now it is almost time
       to bring <u>my everything</u>
       with me, in me,
       to Your wise and understanding heart,

           my God.

They Humor Me

They don't understand
　　　what I want.

　　　　Or,

They ignore
　　　what I ask for.

Instead,

　　　they do (or don't do)
　　　what *they* think I need.

When
　　　I try to insist,
　　　or protest,

They
　　　ever so kindly
　　　humor me.

Maybe they have other things on their mind.
Maybe I'm not clear about my needs.

But this I know:

　　　I am clear to You.
　　　Let me know Your presence,

　　　　　　my God.

This Minute

If I am
the way I should be
because of what's wrong with me,
what have I to give anyone?

That's a hard one.

So I think about it.

       What did I ever—really—
       have to give anyone?

           This minute.
           This minute in this context.
           This minute with what it contained.
           This minute of my presence,
                and theirs.

               So I have come to see
               that what I can give You is
               all and only what I ever did:

               this minute of my presence to You,
               and Your presence to me,

                        my God.

Time

As my mind and heart roam about my life
I see again
how busy
I've been.

      Now, it seems, all I have
      is time.

      I don't have to
      do anything . . .
      (except, some tell me,
      to "get well."
      I'm not so sure
      I'm going to do that.)

So,
at long last,
we have
unhurried time
to be together,

                  my God.

Too Much

I can manage *this,*
or *that,* or the *other thing.*
      ONE at a time.
      NOT all at once!

When *he* comes in to visit,
before *she* leaves,
and then the *phone* rings . . .

It's just too much
for me to manage
all at once.

I get frustrated, maybe
muddled, and irritable.

      I <u>know</u>
      it's not their fault,
      nor mine.

            Help me
            make friends with
            my weakness—
                  and, perhaps,
            be able, peacefully, to
            introduce Weakness
            to my other friends,

                  my God.

Useless?

I'm so sick.
I'm no good for anyone.
I'm useless.
That's what I am: useless!

That's what I think.
That's how I feel.

Until . . .

Until I realize the best part of my life,
the best part of *me,*
is when I love.

Useless as I am for other things,
I still can pick people to love.

Each time I receive a medication,
    I can cover someone with love.
Each time I receive a sip of water,
    I can bathe someone in love.

It's really no surprise,
        is it?
Love always is possible,
Love always is present,
because of You,

        my loving God.

What Do I Do with This?

How many times in my childhood
have I asked:
>"What's this for?"
>"What do I do with it?"

How many times later in my life
>- in times of trouble
>- in times of plenty
have I asked:
>"Why?"
>"What do I do with this?"

Did anyone, along the way,
ever say:
>"Why do you have to do anything?"
>"Enjoy it!"
>"Live the mystery of it!"

>>*And now,*
>>*with the way I am,*
>>*(and all that <u>that</u> means!)*
>>*is*
>>*"Live the mystery of it!"*
>>*Your answer,*

>>>>my God?

What If?

The "What ifs . . ."
of my life
> trouble me,
> intrigue me,
> weary me.

All I can do now is *wonder.*
> - *wonder* at the pieces coming together at last.
> - *wonder* at what I'm seeing, as for the first time.
> - *wonder* at what doesn't matter, anymore.
> - *wonder* at this whole business of dying.

> *And, most of all,*
>> - wonder *what it will be like*
>> *when we meet, at last,*

> my wonderful God.

What Will It Be Like?

When I die
      - will that be the end of everything? . . . or,
      - will I have to suffer for what I've done?
      . . . for the good things I've left undone? . . . or
      - if there is heaven, will it be right away? . . . and
      - will I be again with those who went ahead of me—
      . . . the ones I loved so much . . .
      . . . the ones I've never met, but would like to?

      I don't know.

      But I do know
            You
            are the
            Holy One.
            You
            love me
            unconditionally,
            and as I am.

      So I trust You—
      no matter what it will be like—
      I trust You,
      as I wait to meet You,

                  my God.

Who Am I?

I used to think I knew
      who I was.
If anyone asked me,
      I'd say, " . . . . . ."

    Now
    I'm not so sure.

    My family is saying . . .
    Those who take care of me are saying . . .
    Visitors are saying . . .
    Some people are remembering . . .

How I *come across* to people, and
how I *feel inside* don't always match.

    What *is* the truth of me?

    I suppose I see only bits and pieces,
        "as in a glass, darkly,"
    of You—in whom I trust—

                my God.

Wonder

I wonder about
      my family members,
      my friends and colleagues
      who died before me,
      especially _____.

They say we'll meet again,
      and happily,
      in the life
      into which I am being born.

Will we?

And if we do,
      How will *they* be?
      How will *I* be?
      What will it be like?

           More than ever before,
           I wonder:

               Is it true?
               Is it really true,

                  my God?

Words!

Words!
>So many.
>So fast.
>So insistent.

>>*Talking* wears me out.
>>*Listening* wears me out.
>>*Thinking* wears me out.

>>*I am worn out.*

Now,
>What's left of me?
>I am! Indeed, I am!
>Shorn of talking, of listening,
>>of thinking,
>I am.

>>*And so, simply,*
>>*what I bring You*
>>*is me,*

>>>my God.

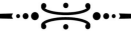

Why Am I Afraid to Die?

Well,
I haven't ever done it before!

Maybe—

        because it seems
        so—*final.*

Perhaps—

        I've never let myself
        really think through
        what I say I believe
        about death and resurrection.

                Help me
                <u>understand</u> and <u>accept</u>,
                and even <u>be glad in</u>
                all those things
                I've been saying I believe.
                Especially in eternal life
                with You,

                        my God.

Why Can't I Die?

Why
can't
I die?

I'm tired of pain.
I'm TIRED.

As far as I can tell
I've lived my life
      as well as (mostly)
      and as long as (it seems)
      it's meant to be.

So why can't I die?

> *Might it be,*
> *just might it be,*
> *that somehow*
> *my living a little longer*
> *is RIGHT?*
> *Right for me,*
> *right for them,*

            my God?

Right Side Up!

My world *is* right side up!

My life *is* right side up!

My dying *is* right side up!

I am right side up!

It is enough.

- It is enough to be here.
- It is enough to be as I have been.
- It is enough to be as I am.

Not only is it enough,

it is right and good

to be, as I am,
suffused with your loving presence,

to be
here
now
in each other's presence,

my God.

An Invitation
to those who are seriously ill
and to those who take care of them

What would you like to see added to *Right Side Up!* that was not included in it?

_____

_____

_____

_____

Have you written a prayer, a poem, a reflection about what it's like for you? Do you think others who are going through what you are going through would be helped by what you have learned? If so, would you send us a copy and let us know if we can use it. Please send a copy of this form along with your reflection.

Name: _____

Address: _____

_____

Phone: _____

Send to:

Sharon Cruse, Assistant Editor
Islewest Publishing
4242 Chavenelle Drive
Dubuque, IA 52002